mondrian

ON THE HUMANITY OF ABSTRACT PAINTING

mondrian

ON THE HUMANITY OF
ABSTRACT PAINTING

Meyer Schapiro

GEORGE BRAZILLER   NEW YORK

Published in the United States in 1995 by George Braziller, Inc.

"On the Humanity of Abstract Painting": from *Proceedings of the American Academy of Arts and Letters and the National Institute of Arts and Letters,* second series, no. 10, Blashfield Address. Copyright © 1960. Reprinted with permission.

"Mondrian: Order and Randomness in Abstract Painting," Copyright © 1978 by Meyer Schapiro.

Both essays originally printed in *Modern Art: 19th & 20th Centuries (Selected Papers, Vol. II),* published in 1982 by George Braziller, Inc.

For information, please write to the publisher:

George Braziller, Inc.
60 Madison Avenue
New York, New York 10010

Library of Congress Cataloging-in-Publication Data:

Schapiro, Meyer, 1904—
    Mondrian: on the humanity of abstract painting /
    Meyer Schapiro.
      p. cm.
    ISBN 0-8076-1370-3
      1. Painting, Abstract.   2. Mondrian, Piet, 1872–1944—
Criticism and interpretation.   I. Title.
ND196.A2S33 1995   94-38797
759.9492—dc20   CIP

Designed by Lundquist Design

Printed and bound in Hong Kong

Contents

■

ON THE HUMANITY OF ABSTRACT PAINTING

■

ON THE HUMANITY OF ABSTRACT PAINTING

(1960)

The notion of humanity in art rests on a norm of the human that has changed in the course of time. Not long ago only the heroic, the mythical, and religious were admitted to high art. The dignity of a work was measured in part by the rank of its theme.

In time it became clear that a scene of common life, a landscape, or still life could be as great a painting as an image of history or myth. One discovered too that in the picturing of the nonhuman were some profound values. I do not mean only the beauty created by the painter's control of color and shapes; the landscape and still life also embodied an individual's feeling for nature and things, his vision in the broadest sense. Humanity in art is therefore not confined to the image of man. Man shows himself too in his relation to the surroundings, in his artifacts, and in the expressive character of all the signs and marks he produces. These may be noble or ignoble, playful or tragic, passionate or serene. Or they may be sensed as unnameable yet compelling moods.

At the threshold of our century stands the art of Cézanne, which imposes on us the conviction that in rendering the simplest objects, bare of ideal meanings, a series of colored patches can be a summit of perfection showing the concentrated qualities and powers of a great mind. Whoever in dismay before the strangeness of certain contemporary works denies to the original painting of our time a sufficient significance and longs for an art with noble and easily read figures and gestures should return to Cézanne and ask what in the appeal of his weighty art depends on a represented human drama. Some of his portraits, perhaps—although to many observers, accustomed to the affability of old portraiture, Cézanne's appeared only a few decades ago mask-like and inhuman, a forerunner of the supposed loss of humanity in twentieth-century art. But are those portraits by Cézanne greater for us, more moving, even more dramatic, than his pictures of fruit and rumpled cloth?

The humanity of art lies in the artist and not simply in what he represents, although this object may be the congenial occasion for the fullest play of his art. It is the painter's constructive activity, his power of impressing a work with feeling and the qualities of thought that gives humanity to art; and this humanity may be realized with an unlimited range of themes or elements of form.

All this has been said often enough; it is granted, and still one clings to Cézanne's apple and doubts in principle that high accomplishment in art is possible where the imagination of colors and forms is divorced from the imaging of the visible world.

Architecture, which represents nothing, is a permanent challenge to that theoretical belief. If a building communicates the values of the home or temple, it is through the splendor of its freely invented forms. However bound to materials and functions, these forms are an expression, not a representation, of the familial or sacred.

The charge of inhumanity brought against abstract painting springs from a failure to see the works as they are; they have been obscured by concepts from other fields. The word "abstract" has connotations of the logical and scientific that are surely foreign to this art. "Abstract" is an unfortunate name; but "nonobjective," "nonfigurative," or "pure painting"—all negative terms—are hardly better. In the nineteenth century, when all painting was representation, the abstract in art meant different things: the simplified line, the decorative, or the flat. For the realist Courbet, a militantly positive mind, it was the imaginary as opposed to the directly seen; to paint the invisible, whether angels or figures of the past, was to make abstract art. But Constable could say: "My limited and abstracted art is to be found under every hedge and lane."

Abstract painting today has little to do with logical abstraction or mathematics. It is fully concrete, without simulating a world of objects or concepts beyond the frame. For the most part, what we see on the canvas belongs there and nowhere else. But it calls up more intensely than ever before the painter at work, his touch, his vitality and mood, the drama of decision in the ongoing process of art. Here the subjective becomes tangible. In certain styles this quality may be seen as a radical realization of the long-developed demand in Western art for the immediate in experience and expression, a demand that, in the preceding art, had found in landscape and still life, and even portraiture, its major themes. If mathematical forms are used, they are, as material marks, elements of the same order of reality as the visible canvas itself. And if a painter ventures to paste on the surface of the canvas bits of objects from without— newsprint and cloth—these objects are not imitated but transported bodily to the canvas, like the paint itself.

An abstract painter entering a room where a mathematician has demonstrated a theorem on the blackboard is charmed by the diagrams and formulas. He scarcely understands what they represent; the correctness or falsity of the argument doesn't concern him. But the geometrical figures and writing in white on black appeal to him as surprising forms—they issue from an individual hand and announce in their sureness and flow the elation of advancing thought. For the mathematician his diagram is merely a practical aid, an illustration of concepts; it doesn't matter to him whether it is done in white or yellow chalk, whether the lines are thick or thin, perfectly smooth or broken, whether the whole is large or small, at the side or center of the board—all that is accidental and the meaning would be the same if the diagram were upside down or drawn by another hand. But for the artist, it is precisely these qualities that count; small changes in the inflection of a line would produce as significant an effect for his eye as the change in a phrase in the statement of a theorem would produce in the logical argument of its proof.

For the artist these elementary shapes have a physiognomy; they are live expressive forms. The perfection of the sphere is not only a mathematical insight, we feel its subtle appearance of the centered and evenly rounded as a fulfillment of our need for completeness, concentration, and repose. It is the ecstatically perceived qualities of the geometrical figure that inspired the definition of God as an infinite circle (or sphere) of which the center is everywhere and the circumference nowhere. In another vein, Whitman's description of God as a square depends on his intense vision of the square as a live form:

> Chanting the square deific, out of the one advancing, out of the sides;
> Out of the old and new—out of the square entirely divine;
> Solid, four-sided (all the sides needed). . . from this side Jehovah am I.

The same form occurred to Tolstoy in his *Diary of a Madman* as an image of religious anguish: "Something was trying to tear my soul asunder but could not do so. . . .

Always the same terror was there—red, white, square. Something is being torn and will not tear."

I shall not conclude that the circle or square on the canvas is, in some hidden sense, a religious symbol, but rather: the capacity of these geometric shapes to serve as metaphors of the divine arises from their living, often momentous, qualities for the sensitive eye.

This eye, which is the painter's eye, feels the so-called abstract line with an innocent and deep response that pervades the whole being. I cannot do better than to read to you some words written from the sensibility to uninterpreted forms by an American over fifty years ago, before abstract art arose.

"How does the straight line feel? It feels, as I suppose it looks, straight—a dull thought drawn out endlessly. It is unstraight lines, or many straight and curved lines together, that are eloquent to the touch. They appear and disappear, are now deep, now shallow, now broken off or lengthened or swelling. They rise and sink beneath my fingers, they are full of sudden starts and pauses, and their variety is inexhaustible and wonderful."

From the reference to touch some of you have guessed, I'm sure, the source of these words. The author is a blind woman, Helen Keller. Her sensitiveness shames us whose open eyes fail to grasp these qualities of form.

But abstract art is not limited to the obvious geometric forms. From the beginning it has shown a remarkable range. It includes whole families of irregular shapes—the spontaneous mark and the patched or spreading spot—elements that correspond in their dynamic character to impulse and sensation and act upon us also by their decided texture and color. Abstract painting shares this variety with modern representational art, and like the latter has already a broad spectrum of styles that recall the Classic, Romantic, and Impressionist by their structure of color and form. The objections to the masters of abstract painting are much like those that have been addressed to the great masters of the nineteenth century: they are too dry, too intellectual, too material, too decorative, too emotional, too sensual and undisciplined. In general, those who reject abstract painting reject, for the same reasons, the newer kinds of representation as well.

Abstract painting is clearly open to a great span of expression; it is practiced differently by many temperaments, a fact that by itself challenges the idea of its inhumanity. We recognize the individual in these works no less than in representations. And in some the artist appears as an original personality with an impressive honesty and strength.

In recent work, puzzled and annoyed observers have found an artless spontaneity that they are happy to compare with the daubings of the monkey in the zoo. This monkey is the fated eternal companion of the painter. When the artist represented the world around him, he was called the ape of nature; when he paints abstractly, he is likened to the monkey who smears and splatters. It seems that the painter cannot escape his animal nature. It is present in all styles.

Although this art has given up representation, it cannot be stressed enough that it carries further the free and unformalized composition practiced by the most advanced artists at the end of the last century in their painting from nature. In older figurative art with complex forms, the composition could be seen as an implicit triangle or circle, and indeed this habit of regarding structure as a vaguely geometric design was responsible for much of the weakness and banality of academic art. In abstract painting such large underlying schemes are no longer present. Even where the elements are perfectly regular, the order of the whole may be extremely elusive. The precise grid of black lines in a painting by Mondrian, so firmly ordered, is an open and unpredictable whole without symmetry or commensurable parts. The example of his austere art has educated a younger generation in the force and niceties of variation with a minimum of elements.

The problem of abstract art, like that of all new styles, is a problem of practical criticism and not of theory, of general laws of art. It is the problem of discriminating the good in an unfamiliar form that is often confused by the discouraging mass of insensitive imitations. The best in art can hardly be discerned through rules; it must be discovered in a sustained experience of serious looking and judging, with all the risks of error.

The demand for order, through which the new is condemned, is often a demand for a certain kind of order, in disregard of the infinity of orders that painters have created and will continue to create. I do not refer here to the desire for a new order, but rather to the requirement of an already known order, familiar and reassuring. It is like the demand for order in the brain-injured that has been described by a great physician and human being, the neurologist Kurt Goldstein: "The sense of order in the patient," he writes, "is an expression of his defect, all expression of his impoverishment with respect to an essentially human trait: the capacity for adequate shifting of attitude."

Looking back to the past, one may regret that painting now is not broader and fails to touch enough in our lives. The same may be said of representation, which, on the whole, lags behind abstract art in inventiveness and conviction; today it is abstract painting that stimulates artists to a freer approach to visible nature and man. It has enlarged the means of the artist who represents and has opened to him regions of feeling and perception unknown before. Abstraction by its audacities also confirms and makes more evident to us the most daring and still unassimilated discoveries of older art.

The criticism of abstract art as inhuman arises in part from a tendency to underestimate inner life and the resources of the imagination. Those who ask of art a reflection and justification of our very human narrowness are forced in time to accept, reluctantly at first, what the best of the new artists have achieved and to regard it in the end as an obvious and necessary enrichment of our lives.

mondrian

ORDER AND RANDOMNESS IN ABSTRACT PAINTING

Plate 1. Mondrian: *Composition*, 1929. Solomon Guggenheim Museum, New York.

Plate 2. Mondrian: *Trees in Moonlight (Trees on a River Bank)*. Escher Foundation, Haags Gemeentemuseum, The Hague.

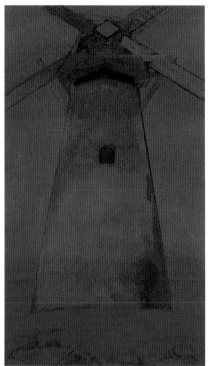

Plate 3. Mondrian: *The Red Mill*, 1911. Haags Gemeentemuseum, The Hague.

Plate 4. Mondrian: *The Church at Domburg*, 1910. Haags Gemeentemuseum, Slijper Collection, The Hague.

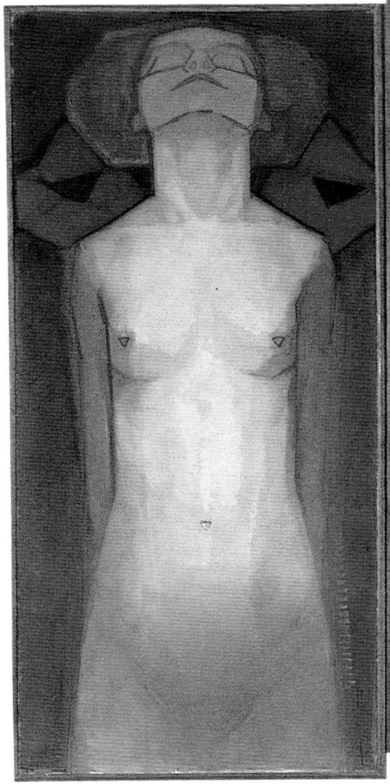

Plate 5. Mondrian: *Evolution (a)*. Escher Foundation, Haags Gemeentemuseum, The Hague.

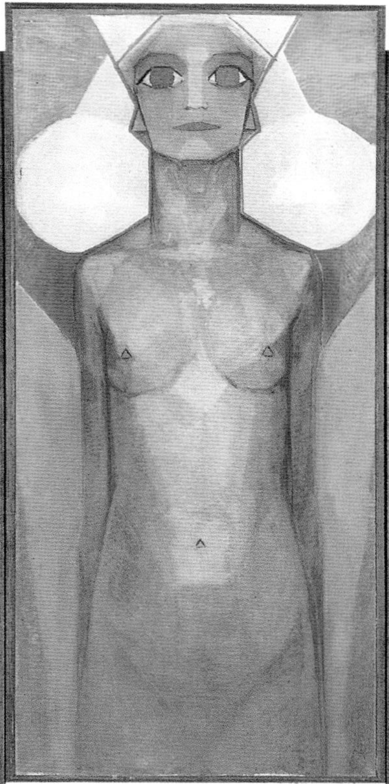

Plate 6. Mondrian: *Evolution (b)*. Escher Foundation, Haags Gemeentemuseum, The Hague.

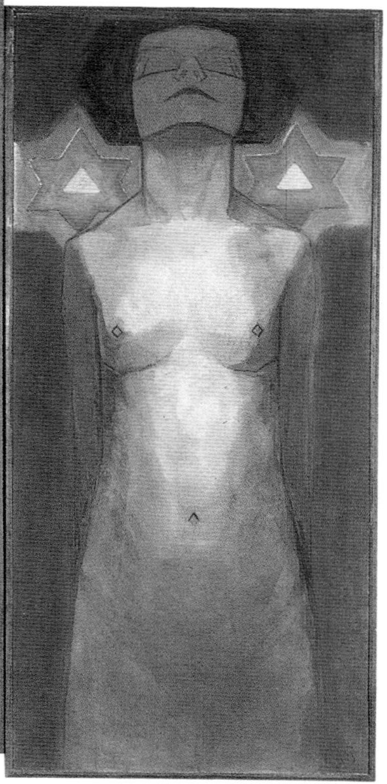

Plate 7. Mondrian: *Evolution (c)*. Escher Foundation, Haags Gemeentemuseum, The Hague.

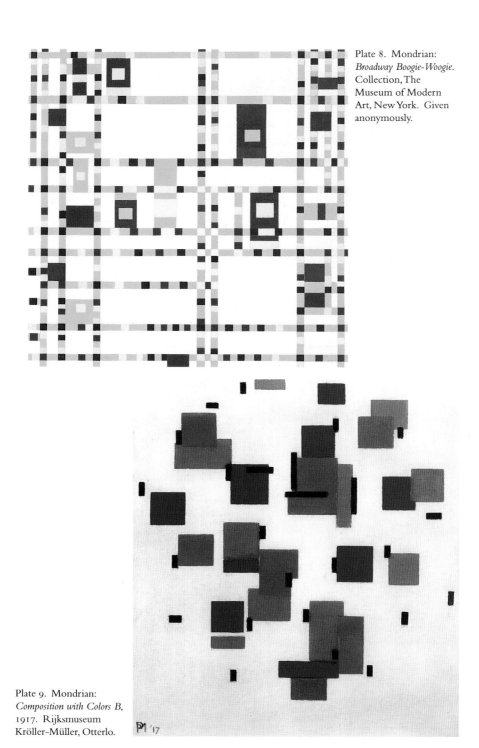

Plate 8. Mondrian: *Broadway Boogie-Woogie*. Collection, The Museum of Modern Art, New York. Given anonymously.

Plate 9. Mondrian: *Composition with Colors B*, 1917. Rijksmuseum Kröller-Müller, Otterlo.

MONDRIAN: ORDER AND RANDOMNESS IN ABSTRACT PAINTING

(1978)

I.

Mondrian's abstract paintings appeared to certain of his contemporaries extremely rigid, more a product of theory than of feeling. One thought of the painter as narrow, doctrinaire, in his inflexible commitment to the right angle and the unmixed primary colors. We learn that he broke with a fellow artist and friend who had ventured to insert a diagonal in that fixed system of vertical and horizontal lines. "After your arbitrary correction of Neo-Plasticism," he wrote to van Doesburg, "any collaboration, of no matter what kind, has become impossible for me," and withdrew from the board of the magazine *De Stijl*, the organ of their advanced ideas.[1]

Yet in the large comprehensive shows of his art one discovers an astonishing range of qualities, a continuous growth from his twenties to his last years in fertile response to the new art of others and to a new milieu. Even while holding strictly to the horizontal and vertical in the painted lines, Mondrian brought back the abhorred diagonal in the frequent diamond shape of a square canvas. Diagonal axes are implicit too in his placing of paired colors. And in his late work he deviated from his long-held principle of the single plane by interlacing the lines to suggest a layered grid in depth. If his abstract paintings of the 1920s and 1930s seem dogmatically limited in their straight forms, these constant elements, through carefully pondered variation of length, thickness, and interval, compose a scale of forces that he deploys in always individual combinations. When studied closely, the barest works, with only a few units, reveal his canny finesse in shaping a balanced order; that variety in the sparse and straight is a ground of their continuing fascination (Pl. 1). One need not analyze that structure, however, to sense its precision and strength. These qualities come to the eye directly like the harmony of a Greek temple. His gravely serious art unites in its forms the large regularities of architecture as a canonical constructed order with a complexity of relations inherited from the painting of nature and the city scene. The persisting white field, in heightened contrast to the black lines, is a luminous ground—it has what may be called after Keats: "the power of white Simplicity"—and, in its division by those lines, provides a measure of the rhythm of the enclosing rectangles.

Like Picasso's art, Mondrian's would have to be characterized very differently according to one's choice of a particular phase as typical. Before the constructive abstract art by which he is best known, his works had been in turn impressionistic, romantic, lyrical, visionary, and symbolic; and in his last years, at seventy, after that severely intellectual style, his paintings became surprisingly sensuous and elated. In assimilating before 1914 the most advanced art of his time, he stood out unmistakably as a painter with his own qualities and powers. Moving from Holland to Paris and later to London and New York, this ascetic artist reacted to each new environment with a quiet enthusiasm, inventing new features that transformed the face of his art. When he worked in the style of Picasso and Braque from 1911 to 1913, he was not far behind them, having absorbed the most recent stage of their rapidly evolving art, and was soon able to move on to more strictly abstract forms of his own invention. Mondrian's warm embrace of Cubism was the more surprising since he was forty then, with a long-matured practice that would have seemed to discourage the change to a style so different in principle from his own. Even more remarkable is that in adopting this challenging art from painters younger than himself, he derived from it conclusions still more radical, which were to stimulate and guide painters in Europe and America in the following decades. His later work was an outcome of reflection and a firm will to rigor, in keeping with a philosophizing habit and long-meditated ideals. Few artists in our century have displayed so ardent a growth.

2.

Mondrian wrote in more than one article that his goal was to achieve an art of "pure relations." These, he believed, had been "veiled" in older painting by the particulars of nature that could only distract the viewer from the universal and absolute in art, the true ground of aesthetic harmony.

I wish in this essay to explore closely several of his abstract works in order to bring into clearer sight the character of those "pure relations" and to show their continuity with structures of representation in the preceding art. For this a minute analysis is necessary. It may be tedious or seem superfluous to one who grasps with feeling the order of a work of Mondrian on immediate view. I shall risk it in the belief that it will also bring us nearer to his sensibility and thought.

In a painting of 1926 in the Museum of Modern Art labeled *Composition in White and Black* (Fig. 1), what seems at first glance a square set within a diamond square—a banal motif of decorators and doodlers—becomes to the probing eye a complex design with a subtly balanced asymmetry of unequal lines. We see the square as partly covered and extending into an imaginary field beyond the diamond canvas. If modeling and perspective have been given up, another cue for depth comes into play in this flat painting on the impenetrable plane of the canvas: the overlapping of forms. The intercepting edge advances and

Figure 1. Mondrian: *Painting I (Composition in White and Black)*, 1926. Collection, The Museum of Modern Art, New York. Katherine S. Dreier Bequest.

the intercepted square recedes as if passing underneath the edge. The whole appears then as a cropped representation of an object in a three-dimensional space. The missing parts are cut off from view at the limits of the diamond field. Only at the upper left corner of the square is the angle closed; but its vertical and horizontal lines cross at that point and are prolonged just enough for us to suppose that what we first perceived as a partly masked square belongs to a larger whole, a lattice or grid formed by bars of varied thickness.[2] We are induced by that single crossing to imagine a similar completion of the other bars and their continuity beyond the square. The black grid seems to exist in a space between the plane of the diamond and the white voids enclosed by the painted bars.

Even if we fix our attention on the canvas as a limited plane surface with a painted set of flat marks complete in themselves as a balanced asymmetric design, another mode of spatial intuition is soon aroused: our habitual response to recognizably incomplete forms. The black bars are envisioned unreflectively as parts of a whole continuing beyond the limits of the overlapping diamond field, although no familiar object has been depicted (unless we regard the thick lines of the "abstract" square as a concrete object like the surface of the canvas itself). Each black line is seen then as an intercepted side of a complete square, just as in a perspective view we identify a partly covered object with its whole. The diamond form of Mondrian's canvas reinforces this effect by the strong contrast of its diagonal edges with the painted lines of the square and by providing between the angles, and especially those above and below, a much greater span than between the parallel lines of the inscribed form. The latter stands out even more decidedly from a larger field in which two lines of the square cross and four triangles are marked as opposing shapes.

Besides, the white surface of the canvas appears to recede as a ground of the salient black grid. We tend to reinforce in perception the separateness of canvas surface and grid and to see the central white field, bounded by the black lines and the intervening edges of the canvas, as a square rather than as the irregular figure it really is. We complete the square because the black bars—as similar, although discontinuous, parts of a familiar configuration— are so much more pronounced than the diagonal corners of that white field, which form coherent parts of a larger pattern of diagonals.

We have before us then the intriguing, in part imagined—one may even say, illusory—appearance of an erect square overlapped at three of its angles by a complete square, a contrasting tilted form. The first square is all verticals and horizontals; the other, all diagonals, an enclosing diamond shape. From this overlay of regular forms results a major figure with seven unequal sides composed of the painted bars and of segments of the unmarked sloping sides of the diamond; and around this unexpected polygon are what appear to be four triangles of unequal area. Two of these have in fact three sides, but the upper and left ones are odd, four-sided figures.[3] The vertical and horizontal bars, too, end in beveled edges. The cropping of an imagined square by a true square yields a whole that is strangely irregular in its varied polygonal parts, yet looks regular, rhythmic, and strictly balanced. The shifting of the square slightly to the right is enough to determine at the other side, at the intersection of the upper horizontal and left vertical bars, a little triangle of black, unique in the work—a shape that resembles, however, the residual white triangles in the right and lower corners of the diamond. That revealing shift, I have noted, marks the sides of the inset square as segments of an extended grid of crossing lines, masked in part by the boundary of the diamond opening or frame. It is not the grid that is asymmetric but the appearance of an externally cropped part of its larger suggested whole. We are led to imagine a viewer so close to the plane of the grid that he can sight only an incomplete segment of one rectangular unit and a corner of a second. The enclosing diamond may be likened to an eye or eyepiece of the beholder, which isolates and frames a visual field; it, too, consists of rectilinear elements like the object sighted, but with contrasted axes. This work of pure design on a flat surface, devoid of representation, does not abolish the illusion of extended space beyond the plane of the canvas or its boundaries, nor the ambiguities of appearance and reality. Nor do its regular features and strictly balanced order exclude the aspect of the incomplete, the random, and contingent.

If Mondrian holds to a set of rules restricting the elements to verticals and horizontals on a single plane and allowing only black and white and the three primary colors that must be contained between those lines and never overflow them, these requirements are not enough to define the structure of the work as an *appearance*. What determines the actual length, position, and thickness of the material lines and the intervals between them? We understand that choice not only through the painter's ardent pursuit of variation; there is also his commitment to an openness and asymmetry that take us beyond the concreteness of the elements and suggest relationships to a space and forms outside the tangible painted surface. Although the lines that are straight bars of considerable thickness seem to belong to a square, measurement will disclose a difference in length between the vertical and horizontal sides. We shall note also that the left and upper lines are thinnest, the bottom line is thicker, the right bar thickest of all. It is as if the square were visualized from the right in a near perspective that gave greater prominence to those two thicker sides.[4] Reading the lines separately as painted black bands on the white surface, we would not say for certain they are segments of one closed figure intercepted by the diagonal edges of the canvas. But no matter how strongly we resolve to see the black bars only as separate painted marks on that limited plane—complete in themselves, unequal, and irregular—we cannot help envisioning a square when we look at them as a whole.[5] The geometric lines together appear then as parts of a virtual object in a larger and deeper space. In this art that seems so self-contained and disavows in theory all reference to a world outside the painting, we tend to complete the apparent forms as if they continued in a hidden surrounding field and were segments of an unbounded grid. It is hard to escape the suggestion that they extend in that virtual space outside.

3.

The root of Mondrian's conception of asymmetrically grouped, segmented forms spanning the field will not be found, I believe, in his earlier paintings from nature nor in his Cubist works in which we already see the reduction of complex natural shapes to a few elementary forms. Picasso and Braque, who had been his inspiring models during the years 1911 to 1913, concentrated in the middle of the canvas a dense, often intricate play of drawn lines— straight, tilted, and curved—with sketchy passages of flecks; together these shape and bind the segments of planes and contours of a reconstituted figure or still life objects as freely joined and disjoined elements of a painterly whole. The simple forms loosen, become sparse, and dissolve toward the edges of the field. If certain lines are carried to the frame and appear to pass behind it, they belong to the background, not to the salient construction. It is rather in the most advanced painting of the late nineteenth century—in works by Monet, Degas, Seurat, and Toulouse-Lautrec—that we find precedents for the pronounced asymmetries in Mondrian's paintings and his extension of foreground lines to the boundary on all sides,

Figure 2. Degas: *At the Milliner's*, 1882. The Metropolitan Museum of Art, New York. Harris Brisbane Dick Fund, 1932.

with their implied continuation beyond. By novel close-up views and by the cropping of objects, those painters make us aware of the actuality of a near and often peripheral observer, as in later photographs and films with odd perspectives that evoke the determining presence of a viewing eye. The spectator is intimated at a localizable point at the side through the angular perspective. Monet has alluded more directly to this sense of a picture as an encountered scene by representing a figure on a high balcony in the foreground, looking at the crowded street below.[6] By sighting the prominent foreground objects from nearby and cutting them abruptly at the edges of the canvas, painters brought the viewer close to the picture space—as if a participant—and marked the resulting strange silhouettes of the very near and incompletely seen as a truth to vision. They produced through those perceptions new patterns of shape and color, almost fanciful in their irregular spottings and arabesques.

An illuminating example is Degas's 1882 picture of a scene in a milliner's shop (Fig. 2). A woman trying on a hat looks intently at an image of herself on the surface of a mirror, as we ourselves look at Degas's pastel. It is a theme of seeing, and more specifically of aesthetic seeing. The woman studies her reflection to judge how the hat composes with her head, how she looks in it, how it looks on her, how each relates to the other. In the background a *modiste*, immobile and detached, holds two other hats for trial. The frame cuts the long mirror below and above. The woman's figure is cut only below and in turn intercepts the baseboard of the wall; the *modiste*, whose features we cannot see, is covered and divided by the mirror and by the vertical edge of the frame at the right—her hand and a hat are incomplete there. What is rendered is a segment of a larger space, as beheld by a very near observer at the right. It has been excerpted by an artist so close to his objects, relative to their size, that with a slight shift of his position they will form a quite different whole. We see the woman looking at the (to us invisible) mirror image that has been excluded from our sight by the painter's viewpoint. Two distinct acts of seeing are projected here: one of a viewer inside the picture, the second of an implied outer viewer—the first without the object she sees, the other no less actual than the first through the near perspective of the depicted objects of his glance. All of these are incomplete, covered in part by the frame and by each other.

Degas's picture of seeing may be taken as a simile of the aesthetic perceptions and self-consciousness that preceded abstract art and prepared its way. The woman at the milliner's is the artist-critic of her own appearance; her object of contemplation—the hat she adjusts on her head—is itself a work of art visualized through its projection on the plane surface of a mirror. Degas's conception is significant for the art of a later time when the painter's need to declare the freedom and self-sufficiency of his art, together with his reflections on an ideal of pure aesthetic seeing and his confidence in the intrinsic plasticity and expressiveness of his medium when freed from all resort to likeness, inspired what in a misleading, but now established, metaphor is called "abstract art." In Degas's pastel the woman is testing the fitness of a work of art that is not at all a representation, yet as a part of her costume will symbolize her individuality and taste in shape and color.

The segmenting of foreground objects at the edges of a field was practiced, of course, in much older Western and Middle Eastern art. But its specific form in the later nineteenth century, with pointed reference to a nearby spectator whose perspective position determines an incomplete and sometimes oddly silhouetted form of a primary object, was something new.[7] It was a mode of painterly vision Mondrian had rarely employed in his landscapes. Before his picture of a mill or tower we hardly think of the viewpoint as that of an ambulant spectator; the arresting object is confronted there in the middle of the canvas (Pl. 3; Fig. 8). The painter has stationed himself straight before it in nature and calls for a corresponding central position of the attentive viewer of the picture. Although we look at a framed image as a balanced whole from a point opposite its central axis, for Degas the pattern of a scene changed decidedly with the artist's distance and his angle of vision in sighting the objects. His virtual presence in the perspective of the pictured scene suggests an attitude toward what catches his eye, whether of detachment or aesthetic interest or cool curiosity in a casual encounter. The objects beheld in the painting intimate in their form both the boundary of that viewer's vision and their own existence in a larger field than is framed, including a space between the canvas and the implied spectator of the original scene. The painting embodies the contingent in a momentary envisionment of the real world, and requires for its reading our fuller knowledge of objects and the conditions of sighting.

I have digressed so long in comparing Mondrian's composition with certain features of Degas's in order to show the continuity of abstract painting with the preceding figurative art, a connection that is generally ignored. If, as Mondrian wrote, he wished to disengage the relations of form that in older art were veiled by a vestment of the material world, how do his "pure relations" differ from the previously masked ones? Are the latter an underlying structure that can be abstracted by divesting a picture of the shapes of particular objects? Are they simply a schematic armature, like the triangle or circle to which an artist adapts his highly articulated natural forms, as disclosed didactically in analytic diagrams of the old masterpieces? No one who has marveled at the beauty of Cézanne's paintings will suppose that their admired relations of form are "veiled" by the less pure forms of material things observed in nature. The effective relations are all there on the surface in the unique strokes of color and are inseparable from the complex shapes given to the represented objects, although we do not analyze the forms in detail any more than we respond to abstract paintings by scanning their structure minutely. Mondrian was surely aware that in those venerated works the old masters considered every detail a necessary part in the order and harmony of the whole.

Yet one may speak of certain relations of the geometric units in Mondrian's paintings as "abstracted" or transposed from the previous art of representation, without assuming that the units themselves are reductions of complex natural forms to simple regular ones. These elements are indeed new, as concrete markings of pigments on the tangible canvas surface with distinctive qualities—straightness, smoothness, firmness—which may be called physiognomic and are grasped as such, rather than as illustrative presentations of the ideal concepts of mathematical or metaphysical thought, although we may use the terms of geometry in talking about them. The position of Mondrian's straight line (which on the diamond field is a bar with mitered ends), its length and thickness, its precise distance from a neighboring line, are no more nor less constitutive of the painting as a unique aesthetic whole than are the complex image-forms that Mondrian wished to supplant by his "pure relations." The new abstract elements of his art are disposed on the canvas in asymmetric and open relationships that had been discovered by earlier painters in the course of a progressive searching of their perceptions of encountered objects in the ordinary world and had been selected for more than aesthetic reasons. In that art of representation, the asymmetry and openness of the whole, which distinguished a new aesthetic, also embodied allusively a way of experiencing directly and pointedly the everyday variable scene—a way significant of a changing outlook in norms of knowledge, freedom, and selfhood. So too one may ask whether Mondrian's use of those compositional relations, although applied to particular geometric units with a characteristic aspect of the elementary, the rigorous, and impersonal as features of an innovating rational aesthetic, perhaps springs from a positive attitude toward that liberating outlook. One cannot read Mondrian's writings without becoming aware of his desire to integrate in a utopian spirit his theory of art with the whole of social life and the promise of a more general emancipation through an advancing modernity.

4.

Mondrian applied the principle of an open asymmetric grid also on his more usual oblong canvas, but with a decidedly architectural effect through the strict accord of the painted lines and the parallel edges of the field. The example I show here was done in 1935 (Fig. 3) and then redone on the same canvas a few years later (Fig. 4).[8] In both states two long lines reaching from top to bottom divide the surface into three subfields like the bays of a tall façade. One of these lines is in the middle of the canvas; with the line at the left, it bounds a central space open at the upper and lower ends. The three bays are successively narrower from right to left, as on a façade seen in perspective from the right. The effect may also be read as a schema of two separate neighboring constructions with an open space between them, each extending indefinitely on three sides and intercepted asymmetrically in the view by

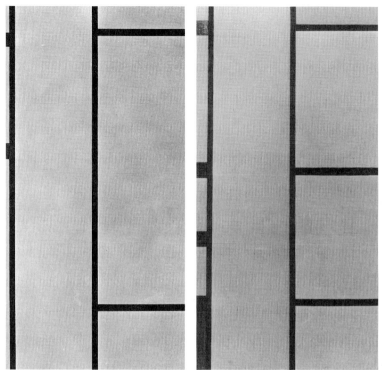

Figure 3. Mondrian: *Composition*, 1935. (First state of Figure 4.) Reproduced in *Cubism and Abstract Art* (New York: Museum of Modern Art, 1936).

Figure 4. Mondrian: *Composition*, 1936–42. Collection of Mr. and Mrs. Burton Tremaine, Meriden, Connecticut.

an imposed windowlike frame. In either reading, a symmetry latent in the central vertical line is revoked by the partitioning of the canvas into three unequal fields. The division of the lateral bays by shorter horizontal bars that bound rectangular spaces of distinctly contrasted areas and proportions reinforces the asymmetry while serving also to balance the inequalities of the two halves of the canvas. All these sub-rectangles are open at one or two sides.

Mondrian was dissatisfied, I suppose, with the first state, for in undertaking to change it toward 1942 he did not simply compose a variant on another canvas, but retouched the original (Fig. 4). In adding horizontals—one at the right and two at the left—he brought the divisions of both bays into closer alignment and introduced a more legible rhythmic order in the proportions of the white spaces on the two sides. The horizontal has been reinforced relative to the vertical, as in other paintings of his last years. A new factor of asymmetry and contrast in the balance of the two halves of the canvas is the accenting of the rectangles in diagonally opposite corners by the addition of color.

This work, too, like the square in the diamond square, may be set instructively beside a composition from the preceding figurative art: a lithograph made in 1895 by Bonnard, an artist of Mondrian's generation who remained faithful to painting from the visible until the end of his life (Fig. 5). In the balanced rendering of beheld objects, all straight-lined, Bonnard's work marks an advanced stage in the passage to an abstract style with asymmetry and open, intercepted forms. Here again the subject is taken from the sphere of art. It is a window view of buildings, geometric in form, that appears as a segment of an extended grid, and that includes the

Figure 5. Bonnard: *View from Window*, 1895. Lithograph. The Metropolitan Museum of Art, New York. Harris Brisbane Dick Fund, 1932.

observer's space. In that vision of architecture, some details are cropped; others, like the upper windows of the distant house, are complete. Although not composed with Mondrian's economy and rigor, the vertical and horizontal are felt throughout as distinct elements of a constructed pattern as well as of the perceived reality. The field is partitioned by the lines of the casement and its sill and by the walls and roofs of the buildings beyond. Both the grid of the large window and the small panes in the distance are contrasted with the white surface between those black lines and spots. There are, however, beside the diagonals of the casement and the emerging roof in the lower left corner of the window view, some loose freehand touches and streaks, a gradation and blending of small picturesque detail, while Mondrian admits in his armature only strict orthogonals, the firm lines of his basic directions.

I do not mean to imply by this comparison that Mondrian's work is a stylized reduction of his vision of an actual scene with buildings. It is a new construction on the canvas, independent of a particular building or site, and has its own canonical elements subject to rules of design he has set himself. But these requirements entail for him, as I have said, certain relationships of form already conceived in recent figurative art. At the same time Mondrian shares with advanced architects an ideal of form supposedly inherent in the nature of their art, its materials, and goals, together with a taste for the simple, the regular, and the asymmetrically balanced as the rational outcome of those

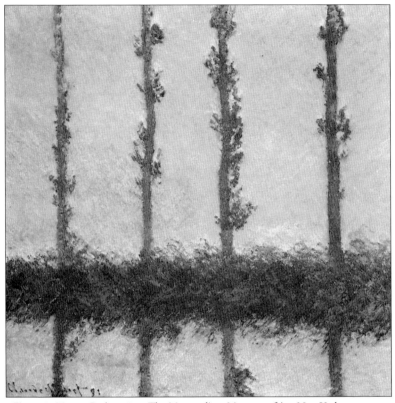

Figure 6. Monet: *Poplars*, 1891. The Metropolitan Museum of Art, New York.

inherent conditions. In opposing the "pure" relations in his art to the "veiled" ones in representations, Mondrian agreed with the purist architects who wished to exclude from their buildings all ornament and preconceived symmetry as a concealment of the working structure—the truly effective elements and relations that made for beauty

46

Figure 7. Mondrian: *Trees in Moonlight (Trees on a River Bank)*, 1908. Escher Foundation, Haags Gemeentemuseum, The Hague.

in their art. The affinity of Mondrian and the modern architects was recognized by both.

The extension of parallel verticals to the upper and lower edges of the canvas was also a device of Monet; it fixed for the viewer the artist's close sighting position in the fore-space of his pictured object. In several of his paintings of the façade of Rouen Cathedral the high wall, seen at an angle from nearby, is cut by the frame at the top and sides.[9] The grid effect is more pronounced in his *Poplars* (1891) at the Metropolitan Museum (Fig. 6), although it lacks the asymmetry of the cathedral views. It is a type of subject that had attracted Mondrian in his earlier years. I have no doubt that Mondrian was acquainted with Monet's art, but he was perhaps unaware of that particular canvas by Monet when he painted in 1908 a mysterious expressionistic moonlight scene with five trees aligned in one plane at a riverbank (Pl. 2; Fig. 7).[10] The slender forms are reflected in the water, parallel to the picture surface. Today an observer who knows Mondrian's abstract style cannot help thinking of it when he sees Monet's painting with its evident natural grid intercepted on all four sides, in spite of the difference of mood and Monet's shaggy silhouettes and ever-present brushstrokes and nuanced tones. But in Mondrian's landscape the trees and their reflections are fully contained on the canvas; the forms are more pliant and irregular than Monet's, which seem to continue beyond the edges of the picture-field in a pattern of endless verticals and horizontals.

Other paintings by Mondrian from the time of his versatile experimentation with advanced modern styles—Neo-Impressionist, Fauvist, Expressionist, and Symbolist—shortly before his turn to Cubism in 1912, foreshadow the geometric units of his abstract work but not their segmentation, openness, and asymmetry.[11] It seems to me unlikely, however, that he could have moved from that earlier phase to his compositions of the 1920s and 1930s without having absorbed later, besides Cubist art, the croppings and asymmetries of the Impressionists and their

48

Figure 8. Mondrian: *The Red Mill*, 1911. Haags
Gemeentemuseum, The Hague.

direct successors in near-views and eccentric angular perspectives. His *Red Mill* (Pl. 3; Fig. 8) and 1911 *Church Tower of Domburg* (Pl. 4) are exceptional among his early works in the marked cutting of a tall structure by the upper edge of the canvas.[12] But in those pictures the dominating architectural object looms symmetrically in the middle of the field. In the triptych *Evolution* (Pls. 5, 6, 7; Figs. 9, 10, 11),[13] painted that same year, the rigid centralized figures with the geometric patterning of bodily details and of the symbolic forms in the background recall the *Mill*. The style of that Symbolist triptych may be regarded as an example of Mondrian's growing interest in geometric elements of drawing, which led him perhaps to the curious, whimsical rendering of the nipples and navels as triangles and lozenges.[14] More likely, the stylized treatment of the stiffly frontal, dark, cold-toned nudes, surprising after his intensely colored, impassioned lyrical paintings from nature, was not a purely aesthetic idea. It was deliberately chosen, together with the solemn postures and geometric emblems, to bring out a symbolic content. Besides the distinction of three evolving stages of spirit through the different postures of the three nudes, certain small accompanying features—the erect, inverted, and fused or intersecting triangles—owe their place here less to artistic necessity than to their meaning in the theosophical doctrine to which he adhered then. But the angularities in the drawing of the female nudes, so oddly masculine, and the reduction and

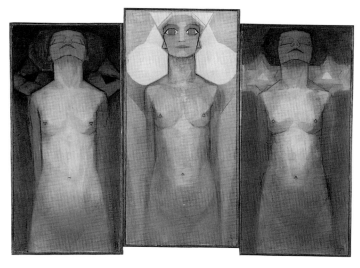

Figure 9. Mondrian:
Evolution (a), 1911.
Escher Foundation,
Haags Gemeentemuseum,
The Hague.

Figure 10. Mondrian:
Evolution (b), 1911.
Escher Foundation,
Haags Gemeentemuseum,
The Hague.

Figure 11. Mondrian:
Evolution (c), 1911.
Escher Foundation,
Haags Gemeentemuseum,
The Hague.

concealment of their hands and feet, may be ascribed as
much to inhibitions with regard to the naked body as to a
spiritualistic ideal of the fusion or balance of the
masculine and feminine, or to his theories about the
vertical and horizontal as similes of spirit and matter
embodied in the two sexes. However one interprets the
change to cold angular forms in this strange triptych, one
ought not to ignore in it the will to a consistent
geometric style that converts both the large and small
details of nature into regular elemental units. It lacks,

however, the distinctive asymmetry and openness of his later abstract works, qualities that relate more to the empirical than to speculative thought.

Yet, if Mondrian's step to Cubism was prepared by his quest for a metaphysical absolute in paintings that were so far from the radical new art of Picasso and Braque in method and idea, it is all the more remarkable that he grasped their aims so surely at the rapidly changing stage of their work when he first encountered it. More pertinent, I believe, in Mondrian's quick response was his earlier practice of Neo-Impressionist and Fauvist styles, with the brushstroke as the discrete unit of painting, whether as a small regular touch or a large emphatic spotting. But in assimilating the Cubist approach he turned away for good from Expressionist pathos and Fauvist intensity as well as from Symbolism and its rhetoric of demonstrative postures, emblems, and spiritualistic dualities, although he retained for a short while such affect-laden subjects as the high church façade and the intricate, wide-branching skeletal tree. If, as has been supposed, the dogma of the exclusive balanced vertical and horizontal in the later work was based on a theosophist conviction formed during his earlier years, its strict application had to wait for his experience of Cubism, an art that freed him from overt symbolic imagery, as well as from lyrical renderings of nature, and turned his mind to a conception of his art as, in essence, a constructive operation with elementary, nonmimetic

Figure 12. Mondrian: *Composition No. 10 (Pier and Ocean)*, 1915. Rijksmuseum Kröller–Müller, Otterlo.

forms. It was an astonishing conversion for an accomplished painter of nature at the age of forty.

5.

Between that Cubist experience and the abstract style with the open grid intervened a stage of abstraction in which Mondrian reverted to features of his pre-Cubist art. In the years 1914 to 1917 he painted a series of works formed of short vertical and horizontal units, many of them tangent or crossed.[15] These black lines or bars, more graphic than painted, fill the surface compactly although with a more scattered effect than the array of parallel colored strokes of his earlier landscapes in a quasi-pointillist technique. Together they shape paradoxically an oval or ellipse without a single curved or diagonal line. In the titles Mondrian gave to certain of those paintings: *Ocean, Pier and Ocean* (Fig. 12), and in the traces of perspective vision, he avowed a tie with direct perception of nature. In an example of 1915 the discrete units become progressively smaller toward the top of the field, and on the central vertical axis of the lower half a distinct series of somewhat longer parallel verticals retains the look of a pier extending into the ocean.[16] Mondrian has translated into his own signs a Neo-Impressionist notation for a view of the sea from a central viewpoint; the dots or strokes of color, which in the paintings of Seurat and his followers were units of both sensation and construction, have been transformed with a delicate calligraphic touch into thin black lines on a white ground with a fine flicker worthy of Seurat's art. Different values of light result from the varying densities of those little marks that suggest the distant wavelets, movement, and texture of the sea. Many years later Mondrian could write of these abstractions: "I felt that I still worked as an Impressionist, and expressed a particular feeling, not reality *as it is*."[17]

The reference to nature disappears in an example of 1917 with thicker, more distinct units (Fig. 13). The

Figure 13. Mondrian: *Composition with Lines*, 1917. Rijksmuseum Kröller-Müller, Otterlo.

rounded space is virtually outlined by a staggered succession of single bars, mainly vertical at the left and right and horizontal at the top and bottom. No straight unit is intercepted by the curved boundary, which is like a round eyepiece through which one sights a field of orthogonal elements. The intermittent contour, flattened at the poles, appears as a sum of the solid rectilinear units. While the single ones at opposite sides of the perimeter form symmetric sets, the bars inside that boundary differ more in length and look chaotically strewn, unordered with respect either to a center or to implicit radii or chords of the circle. Some bars occur singly, some are paired as equal parallels, some touch or cross one or two others, and in several places four and even five or six are in contact, as in *Pier and Ocean,* but with a weight of black that changes the impact of the whole and the strength of contrast to the white ground. These clusters are like molecules, each with a varying number and size of the two kinds of atoms. Yet certain regularities will be found in their seemingly random occurrence. Throughout, one meets only black vertical and horizontal bars (and a few tiny squares) on a common white ground. These fill the space with an almost uniform density, except for a notable decrease toward the flattened top—a lightening most marked along the central axis of the upper half with its loose alignment of single, small units. There is also a long file of vertical bars in the lower half, a little to the right of the central axis, and larger than the irregularly grouped units above. Together, these two sets of verticals reinforce the symmetry of the bars at the rounded edge. Exceptional too is the series of single vertical bars in diagonal file at the lower left, which parallels a similar set on the contour nearby. One cannot say, however, where the varied clusters will turn up. Most of them are asymmetric and some appear highly irregular as composite forms, although built of verticals and horizontals alone. With the single bars, their spotting of the surface determines relatively shapeless, open ground intervals that we do not measure separately by eye, but see together as the common circular field of the assembly of distinct black units, unlike the definite, rhythmically proportioned, white areas enclosed between the black bars in the later abstract works (Fig. 4). Still, there is a statistical order in the clusters as a set. A rough count shows that the frequency of a type of cluster varies inversely as the number of its bars. The singles are the most common; next are the doubles and triples; the clusters of five and six are the fewest of all. There is also a bias in their frequencies in the different horizontal sections of the circle. The largest clusters are almost all in the middle and lowest zones.

In this carefully pondered, yet seemingly random composition of hundreds of variants of a basic unit, we see a novel interplay of contrasts: the vertical and horizontal, their regular and irregular combinations, symmetric and scattered groupings, the qualities of the small unit and the summated whole. Nothing in the form and little in the distribution of the elements inside the contour suggest they are in a circular field. As in the painting of the square within the diamond square (Fig. 1) the simple and regular compose a surprisingly irregular design, so here the elementary vertical and horizontal units shape an aggregate with an irreducible complexity of which the large form approximates a circle. It is a mysterious, fascinating unity. The random and the regular have been balanced so that the random maintains its interest as a quality of the whole, while the elements, small and large, are all visibly constructed of the same kind of regular units, some of them in symmetric relation.

It is hard to imagine how in shaping and filling this circle with several hundred small units Mondrian judged the weight of each one separately in relation to every other in the field and to the simultaneously given whole, as he could do in deciding the precise lengths, intervals, and positions of the few long bars in his later sparse abstractions. He wrote in 1914 of his use of only vertical and horizontal lines that lie "constructed *consciously*, though not by *calculation*, and directed by higher intuition . . . ; *chance* must be avoided as much as *calculation*."[18] Guided by already fixed general constraints on the permitted elements and their relations, the painter could realize experimentally, in a process of trial and error, the balance, order, and harmony of so densely populated a field in appraising by eye with that critical intuition the progressively emerging summated effect or resultant of the immense number of black elements and the indeterminate confluent shapes of the maze of open intervals. His approach to unity was not unlike that of the Impressionists and Neo-Impressionists in achieving the coherence and harmony of a microstructure of countless indistinct points of color. Although Mondrian, in this work of 1917, has cut all evident ties with the natural scene that had supplied him for his painting of *Pier and Ocean* with a model or framework of an order in the perspective and objects of the seascape, he still retained from that older art an experience of composition with very small scattered units. Their density, randomness, and variation recall the Impressionists' free play with contrast, color, and texture in tiny, juxtaposed, and overlaid, sometimes chaotic, touches.

Long before that phase, while still practicing an old-fashioned style in browns and grays, although with an increasingly free sketchy hand, he would dose a greenish meadow with scattered accents of dark and light strokes.[19] Later, toward 1910, in pictures of a tower, a windmill, a lighthouse, and haystacks, and also of a single wide-branching tree, the sky and earth and sometimes the main object are a loose array of multiplied impasto strokes of red and blue aligned in contrasted horizontal and vertical sets.[20] During the same years his beautiful paintings of the *Dunes* show a more minute and refined mosaic technique, obviously indebted to Seurat or his followers.[21]

Although Mondrian's composition of bars suspended in a circle lacks precisely that compactness of the units in Impressionist and Neo-Impressionist paintings where the surface is so often an unbroken weave or crust of tiny overlaid touches of color, there is a type of Impressionist subject that occasioned for Monet and Pissarro patterns of larger scattered elements on a light ground, more like the

Figure 14. Pissarro: *Place du Théâtre Français*, 1898. Los Angeles County Museum of Art, Los Angeles.

aspect of Mondrian's circle. I have in mind their spectacular views of the Paris streets, the first truly modern pictures of a city as a world of crowds in random motion.[22] Pissarro's perspective of the human and wheeled traffic circulating in the irregular *Place du Théâtre Français* (Fig. 14) presents an accidental strewing of figures and vehicles analogous to the multitude of single and clustered bars in Mondrian's abstraction. But on Pissarro's canvas we sense also the motion of the artist's hand and the intentness of his eye scanning the site for its varied tones and contrasts. His sketchy strokes seem to reenact the intermittent movement of the crowd, the carriages, and buses, halting or advancing in their different directions toward and away from us. It is a freshness and liberty of touch in keeping with the nature of the scene as perceived by Pissarro with enjoyment of its changing face, a liberty once valued by Mondrian too but deliberately replaced by a smooth, impersonal execution and strict adherence to the regular vertical and horizontal bars as theoretically grounded, necessary elements of his new art.

We are able to reconstruct, at least in part, certain steps of the process in the painting of 1917 by comparing the final work with an earlier state known through a photograph.[23] The elements then were thinner and longer, not yet solid rectangular bars but graphic lines. The outermost ones were less distinctly a circular contour; they include many complex clusters of crisscrossed lines and are spiky in effect, with loose sections of scaffolding from a phase of Mondrian's Cubist style.[24] While closer in some features to *Pier and Ocean*, the whole lacks altogether the lightness, the delicacy of detail, and perspective suggestions that make the latter so imaginative and lyrical a work. Knowing the direction of Mondrian's growth in the early 1920s toward sparseness and clarity of elements and legible relations, we are interested to note that Mondrian could not rest with that bristling assembly of crossed lines. It was perhaps in reshaping this unsatisfying state that he came to invent the new forms of the

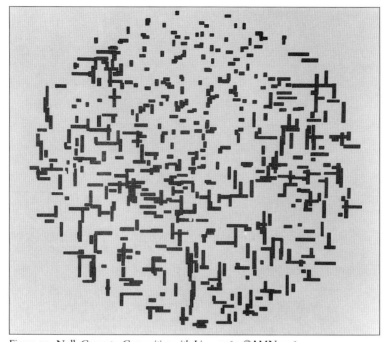

Figure 15. Noll: *Computer Composition with Lines*, 1964. ©AMN, 1965.

composition of 1917. In that change he participated with other leaders of European art in creating the new trend toward the distinctness and legibility of single elements that was to dominate both abstract and figurative painting in the 1920s.

A computer simulation of Mondrian's circular painting permits us to see more sharply by comparison his distinctive order and refinement as a composer. A physicist at the Bell Laboratories, Dr. A. Michael Noll, produced that computer version for a test of artistic perception and judgment with the technical and office staffs as subjects.[25] Analyzing the components of the work with respect to their variable size and position, he programmed the instrument to shape a "reasonably similar" composition— what he regarded as an "equivalent," although admittedly more random. Xerox reproductions of photographs of the original and the simulation (Fig. 15) were shown to the subjects who were asked to indicate their feeling toward abstract art, whether of like, dislike, or indifference, and to answer two questions: which of the works is the computer's? and, which of the two do you "most strongly like or prefer?" Of the hundred members of the combined staffs, only 28 percent identified the computer product correctly and 59 percent preferred it to the other. That judgment of the computer picture was shared by lovers of abstract art—they made up 75 percent of the respondents—and by those indifferent to it, as well as by some who admitted their distaste for that art. The subjects as a group had little or no artistic training. The highest percentage of any subgroup preferring the computer version—76 percent—was of subjects who expressed a liking or even a strong liking for abstract art. Some who preferred the simulation and judged it to be the original described it as "neater," more "varied," "imaginative," "soothing," and "abstract" than Mondrian's work. There was no significant difference between the aesthetic responses of the office employees (one-third of the subjects) and the scientists and engineers of the technical staff, although the latter did somewhat better in identifying the machine-made picture, perhaps because of their familiarity with computers. The ones that liked abstract art and those indifferent to it had the same success in this game of recognition, but from an aesthetic point of view the subjects who disliked the art were the most successful; theirs was the lowest percentage of preference for the simulation.

I believe Dr. Noll was right in explaining the taste for the relatively shapeless computer version by the frequency of randomness in recent abstract paintings and the association of that feature with an idea of the creative in general.[26] The more clearly ordered structure of the true Mondrian appeared then as the attribute of a machine-made work. The vogue of Abstract Expressionist painting that was often identified with the more impulsive, spontaneous-looking products of this varied group of artists, despite some distinctly different individual styles, fixed in the receptive public's mind an image of that art as a heroic formlessness exemplifying a noble inner freedom and resistance to constraints.[27] One ignored the serious concern for coherent form and color among the best of the artists.

The experiment is an evidence of a now common but usually ignored response to abstract painting. While Mondrian and other pioneers of this new art saw the portrayal of objects as an obstacle to experience of purely artistic relations and looked to abstraction as the way to a purified art, we learn from this trial of judgment that the randomness of strewn forms, without likeness to particulars of nature, could be enjoyed as a positive quality in art and preferred in a less accomplished simulation, just as in the past certain features of a represented subject—the various sentiments and associations suggested by them—were attractive to the viewer uneducated in art and blind to the weakness and banality of the work. Randomness as a new mode of composition, whether of simple geometric units or of sketchy brushstrokes, has become an accepted sign of modernity, a token of freedom and ongoing bustling activity. It is alluring in the same degree that technical and aesthetic features in figurative art, found in the works of the masters—microscopic minuteness of detail, smoothness of finish, virtuoso rendering of textures—besides an agreeable subject, could satisfy in mediocre paintings a taste that was insensitive to relationships of a finer order. The artistically immature taste for the imitative, cliché-ridden, often skillful kind of painting, called kitsch, is now directed also to the widely publicized abstract art.

6.

In his last years Mondrian transformed his abstract art through features that revived qualities of Neo-Impressionist painting and its successors—of their color above all. He did not return, however, to the painterly

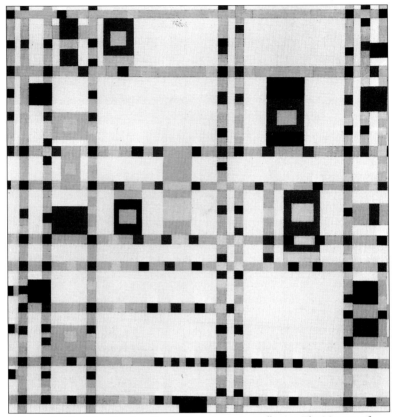

Figure 16. Mondrian: *Broadway Boogie-Woogie*, 1942–43. Collection, The Museum of Modern Art, New York. Given anonymously.

brushstroke or to representation. It was still with his regular constructive elements and dispassionate touch that he created the new style. But he reintroduced also a randomized play of small units and a symmetry of the large as a stabilizing force.

The masterpiece of this final stage he called *Broadway Boogie-Woogie* (Pl. 8; Fig. 16). The title points to the inspiration of music and dance, but without knowing the title, one would think of music in seeing this wonderfully lively, colorful, jazzy canvas.

It is founded on a grid of vertical and horizontal bars, more varied than before in spacing and length. The firm black bands that had been a mainstay for so many years become trains of speckled color; they are divided into small units like the tesserae of a mosaic, mainly yellow alternating with red, grey, and blue. Mondrian, after Monet and Seurat, now excludes black from his palette. The bands appear filmy, bright, and vibrant in the changing sequence of those colors on the white ground and in the recurring contrasts of deep blue and red with the lighter yellow and gray, which on some bars are expanded as longer notes. Even by close scrutiny and with the help of a notation, one cannot transcribe an obvious scheme or rule in the rhythmic succession of those colored notes. One senses only a perpetual permutation, as of beads of the same four colors held together on a common string. The order of the four (and even the coupling of two) on any segment is rarely repeated on the same track. If a particular sequence reappears on a neighboring band—and this is rare—it is in a staggered diagonal relation to the first. Each band is individual through a unique order of the continually permuted colors. We do not discern at a glance the sequence that makes for the difference; the number of units on each complete band—between thirty and forty—is too great to permit one to read the whole distinctly. The notes have been thoroughly shuffled throughout to yield a maximum randomness, while keeping their likeness and coherence as oblong or square units of the same width and family of four colors. Their confinement to the parallel tracks of the grid is a means of order as well as movement.

In contrast to that regularity of axis, larger rectangular blocks of color are inserted, like a syncopating staccato accompaniment, in the intervals of the grid, partly or wholly in contact with it. Certain ones are single units of solid red or blue; some are partitioned by two or three colors; in others a small square of contrasting color is inlaid on the main line as a ground. In several places a color of the larger unit extends across the slender, neighboring bar as if bonded with it. At the lower left, a square of yellow with a central gray spot is mortised into the adjoining bands by its continuity with the yellow squares on the grid. The bonding of the grid with the larger colored rectangles appears at other points and differently in each. The colors of these blocks are the same four as those on the grid; by their greater mass they contribute single forceful beats, like strong chords, to the animation of the whole, and stand out from the grid by their discoordinate grouping and rhythm. They also diversify the white-ground intervals which are broken up rhythmically into smaller, oblong spaces by the encroachments of the inserted blocks. These solid units of color are frequent in the left half of the painting and in the upper part, and fewer but more massive at the right where they are aligned in stepped diagonal sequence.

Although spaced less evenly than in any previous work, the grid as a whole has a somewhat closed and nearly centralized symmetric effect. The corresponding sets of four vertical bars at each side are more compact than the rest of the field, which is distinguished by its broader spaces and is divided by a pair of verticals slightly off-center. Some bars are discontinuous, arrested in midcourse or sooner. It is worthwhile retracing these variations and breaks; they are examples of Mondrian's method as a highly conscious composer. Among the verticals (reading from left to right) the first ends at the third horizontal from the top, the third at the lowest horizontal from the bottom; the sixth stops at the third horizontal, but starts again at the fourth and descends to the lower edge of the canvas; a vertical bar is inserted between the fourth and sixth horizontal; the eighth vertical, too, ends short at the third horizontal; the ninth is interrupted, is resumed twice, and ends well before reaching the eighth transverse band. Among the horizontals the main break is of the seventh, which extends from the second vertical to the sixth; one will notice also, in the lower left, three short bars between the second vertical and the canvas edge. Counting the bars whose ends touch or nearly touch an edge of the canvas, one discovers that there are ten such contacts on the upper edge and eleven at the left, eight at the right and seven below—a choice that effects a diagonal symmetry, in contrast to the dominant vertical symmetry of the grid.

I would not trouble to cite these observations if I did not believe they bring one to see better Mondrian's vigilant planning for variation, balance, and interest. His were not just the moves of an intellectual game or tour de force of painterly construction. Through the rhythm of differences and contrasts of a few colors and lines, with an appearance of both freedom and control in the opposition of the regular and the random, he effects a stirring expression of his delight in sensation and movement.

In this culminating work Mondrian has drawn on his past styles. We see again the stabilizing grid; the molecular scattered units; the repeated arrays of primary color as in his Neo-Impressionist phase; and the composition of large squares applied as separate planes of color in paintings of 1917 (Pl. 9).[28]

There is also in this work a striking departure from Mondrian's long commitment to the single plane. At certain crossings of the grid, he has extended the color of the square unit to a neighboring unit of one or the other band. Distinguished by this accent, one band seems to come forward in crossing its perpendicular. The grid appears then as a network of interlaced bands that follows no regular scheme; it is an arbitrary, occasional entwining like the elusive intersection of planes in Cubist paintings by Picasso and Braque in 1911 and 1912.[29]

While Mondrian's abstract paintings of the 1920s and 1930s have an architectural effect with an impressive stability and strength, the surprise of *Broadway Boogie-Woogie* lies in its movement and colorful visual music. The reversion to his earlier styles clearly served a new expressive intent.

In conceiving *Broadway Boogie-Woogie*, Mondrian could well have been inspired by the sights of New York, the dazzling night spectacle of its high buildings with their countless points of light, and in particular the moving illumined signs at Times Square. He had been prepared for this new conception by his enjoyment of Paris where, on first encountering jazz and modern popular dance in the 1920s, he defended them against detractors. In Paris he discovered, besides Cubist painting, the beauty of a big city as a collective work of art and its promise of greater freedom and an understanding milieu. Shortly before coming to New York he had disclosed a new inspiration in paintings with more complex grids, which he called *Place de la Concorde* and *Trafalgar Square*— the forerunners of the interwoven grid in *New York City* and *Broadway Boogie-Woogie*. But his pleasure in the spotting of bright colors had been awakened before his Paris days. I have noted earlier that in 1909 and 1910, in rural scenes of Holland, often with a single dominant object, he had practiced a style of distinct touches of intense colors, less compact and less regular in form, to be sure, and in some works a more dense mosaic derived from Seurat. In his writings he had acknowledged the importance of Neo-Impressionism for the growth of abstract art. It appears that in his old age a warmer side of his nature, emotion suppressed in his search for an intellectual absolute, was released with a new freedom through his experience of a welcoming American milieu.

The elated spirit of the last paintings reminds one of the last works of Matisse in the 1950s. The convergence of these two masterly artists of the same generation, so different in temperament and culture, invites us to meditate on the old age of the two men. For Matisse it was a rejuvenation, while Mondrian achieved then a youthfulness he had not shown as a young painter. Both had been attracted by jazz and had admired the American city, but it was Mondrian who shaped in *Broadway Boogie-Woogie* a captivating pictorial equivalent of the stirring rhythms and sounds of the mid-Manhattan scene. Matisse, from another standpoint, found in geometrical abstraction and in floral plant patterns a new expression of his abiding delight in color and exotic decorative forms. Those designs, despite some ingenious small deviations from regularity, preserve the traditional syntax of ornament as a system of symmetries and repeats. Mondrian was never freer and more colorful, and closer to the city spectacle in its double aspect of the architectural as an endless construction of repeated regular units and of the random in the perpetual movement of people, traffic, and flashing lights.

NOTES

This paper is an enlarged version of a talk on Mondrian at the symposium at the Guggenheim Museum on October 9, 1971, during the centennial exhibition of the painter's works. The essential points go back to lectures on Mondrian and other abstract painters in my courses on twentieth-century art at Columbia University and in lectures elsewhere since the late 1930s.

1   The letter of 1924 is quoted by Michel Seuphor, *Piet Mondrian, Life and Work*, Abrams, New York, n.d. (1956), p. 149.

2   In some later paintings of the square on the diamond field no line of the square crosses another, so that a grid is not suggested. See Seuphor, p. 392, nos. 408, 410, and the catalogue of the *Centennial Exhibition*, Guggenheim Museum, New York, 1971, p. 193, no. 111 (1930); p. 196, no. 114 (1933). (The catalogue is cited hereafter: *Centennial*, 1971.)

3   With a rotation of 90° the diamond will appear as an erect square; the enclosed square will assume the appearance of a cropped diamond; and the residual triangles will form a nearly symmetric set with respect to a vertical axis.

4   In another painting of a square in a diamond (*Composition with Yellow Lines*, 1933, Haags Gemeentemuseum, The Hague, reproduced by Seuphor, p. 392, no. 410), it is the upper and left bars that are thickest and longest, as if in a perspective from above and the left.

5   To test the effect of interception and openness on the appearance of the painted bars on their white ground, replace the diamond by an erect square of the same size. The bars with their beveled ends will seem then to float on that surface as separate units. As a set of discrete elements they will lack the expansiveness and tension arising from the appearance of a square intercepted by an enclosing form, and the composition as a whole will lose its compactness and strength of contrast.

6   In the painting of the *Boulevard des Capucines* in the Marshall
    Field III Collection, reproduced in color by William C. Seitz,
    Claude Monet, New York, 1960, frontispiece.

7   An approach to this modern use of perspective will be found in
    paintings of interiors by Dutch artists of the seventeenth century.
    An example is Vermeer's *Love Letter* in the Rijksmuseum,
    Amsterdam (see Lawrence Gowing, *Vermeer*, New York, 1953, pl.
    62), where the two figures are seen fully enough through a
    doorway whose cropped sides, without visible top or bottom,
    frame the subject in the room beyond. More like the modern
    conception is a picture of the *Interior of the Church of Saint Bavo in
    Haarlem* (Fig. 17), painted by Pieter Saenredam (1597–1655) in
    1635. In the near foreground he represents the great round pillars

Figure 17. Saenredam: *Interior of the Church of Saint Bavo in Haarlem*, 1635. The National
Gallery, London.

of the nave from a position in the aisle directly in front of the left-most pillar and so close that we see of it only a short segment spanning the height of the broad canvas. It is also cut abruptly by the frame at the left and, with two other pillars beside it, blocks much of the interior space. Those two pillars, segmented and unevenly spaced in the middle and at the right—like the verticals in Mondrian's rectangular canvases (see Figs. 3 and 4)—repeat the strong vertical of the first. The smooth, white walls of the church, the cool light, the clear contrast and balance of the dominant verticals and horizontals, and the unornamented Gothic form could lead one to invoke the name of Saenredam as a native ancestor of Mondrian's abstract taste (as has been done by Jean Leymarie in his book *La Peinture Hollandaise*, Skira, Geneva and Paris, 1956, p. 150; it is interesting to note also that H. P. Bremmer, one of the first Dutch critics to appreciate Mondrian's abstract works, was later to write a monograph on Saenredam; that painting of Saint Bavo's church has been reproduced by Thomas Hess in his book *Abstract Painting, Background and American Phase*, New York, 1951, p. 22, fig. 12, as an example of an older Dutch artist's taste for abstract form). A large diamond plaque hangs from the middle pillar; it is the escutcheon of a deceased, common in Dutch church interiors in the seventeenth century.

Saenredam seems not to have repeated this daring perspective, which remains exceptional among the paintings of church interiors by Dutch artists. But it is a noteworthy anticipation of an artistic idea of nineteenth-century painters, in accord with advanced tendencies of other Dutch artists toward the near-view and the theme of sighting. Jantzen, in his thoughtful, ground-breaking study of the painting of architectural views in the Netherlands in the seventeenth century, judged that work by Saenredam to be a bungled experiment: "an arbitrary slice of space, something accidental and unstructured. How unsuccessful is the whole in its wide format! The three pillars look as if they were beheaded with a sickle . . . Saenredam himself recognized the failure of this solution" (Hans Jantzen, *Das niederländische Architekturbild*, Leipzig, 1910, p. 81). In the next year he painted another view of the same interior as a tall, narrow composition framed symmetrically by two pillars and their arch, with a central view from a greater distance (Jantzen, pp. 81–82 and pl. 33). I may call attention also to diamond-shaped escutcheons in later pictures of church interiors by Emanuel de Witte (Jantzen, pls. 61, 62), with a single vertical bar at the left of center crossed by a horizontal, which recall a painting by Mondrian reproduced by Seuphor, p. 392, no. 492.

8   The first state was reproduced in Alfred Barr's pioneering catalogue of the great exhibition of *Cubism and Abstract Art* held at the Museum of Modern Art in 1936, p. 152, no. 158 (186).

9   Cf. the example in the Boston Museum, *Façade at Sunset*, reproduced by W. C. Seitz, *Claude Monet*, p. 143 (color plate), and one in the Metropolitan Museum, Seitz, p. 38, fig. 49.

10   See *Centennial*, 1971, p. 106, no. 22, and also p.15 for a photograph of the site, with the treetops cut by the upper edge of the print, as in Monet's *Poplars*.

11   It is interesting to note also in his pre-Cubist paintings examples of the grid as a represented form. Looking back from his abstractions to a picture in the Museum of Modern Art of a windmill painted about 1900 (Seuphor, p. 228), one is struck by the crisscross of the mill vane, a fence, the window of a door, and of their reflections in the water. But these are minor elements in the rendering of a landscape where larger shapes, sketchy and patched, are more pronounced. The grid here is a pattern of single, isolated objects, not an organizing principle of the entire painting.

12   Seuphor, p. 128 and p. 127; cf. also *Church at Zouteland* (1909–10) p. 124 (color plate). He had already painted windmills in this precisely centralized position in 1908 (p. 111, nos. 27, 28), but they lack the evident formality of placing that distinguishes the later examples.

13 Ibid., p. 129, color plate.

14 The triangular nipples and navel of the first nude point downward like the large pair of triangles above her shoulders; they are presumably attributes of the material, the earthy. In the second figure, with large, wide-open, staring eyes—signs of spirit—all the triangles are erect. In the third nude, who apparently symbolizes the fusion of matter and spirit or their balance and holds her head high with tightly closed eyes as if to signify inwardness and contemplation, the three little triangles have become lozenges. Above her shoulders are paired the intersecting triangles, a theosophist emblem.

15 Reproduced by Seuphor, nos. 223–39, pp. 316–77.

16 Ibid., no. 239, p. 377; for a color plate, see *History of Modern Painting from Picasso to Surrealism*, Skira, Geneva, 1950, p. 117.

17 *Towards the True Vision of Reality*, an autobiographical essay, quoted by Seuphor, p. 120. See also *History of Modern Painting*, p. 199.

18 From a letter to H. P. Bremmer quoted by Joop Joosten in *Centennial*, 1971, p. 61.

19 Seuphor, p. 49, color plate (c. 1902).

20 *Illustrated in Centennial*, 1971, catalogue nos. 31, 32, 34, 37–39, 41, 42, 44, and by Seuphor, pp. 75, 95.

21 Seuphor, p. 376, no. 219; cf. also nos. 218–21 and p. 375, nos. 210, 212; *Centennial*, 1971, p. 120, no. 37 and p. 121, no. 38.

22 I have in mind particularly Monet's paintings of the *Boulevard des Capucines* and the *Boulevard des Italiens*. See note 6 above.

23 It is reproduced by Joop Joosten in his article in *Centennial*, 1971, p. 65, fig. 15.

24 This work also brings to mind his minutely detailed studies of single flowers, drawn between 1906 and 1910, mainly chrysanthemums with a circle of densely packed, slender, raylike petals seen *en face*, overlapping, and often unkempt. (Seuphor, pp. 368–71, nos. 128–52, 158–71, 177–78, 187–91, 196–204, 235–43, 249–62, 294–301.)

25 A. Michael Noll, "Human or Machine: A Subjective Comparison of Piet Mondrian's *Composition with Lines* (1917) and a Computer-Generated Picture," *The Psychological Record* 16, 1966, pp. 1–10.

26 An example is the figure preference test for "creativeness," published by Frank Barron ("The Psychology of Imagination," *Scientific American* 199, Sept. 1958, pp. 150 ff.). Subjects were shown two sets of "abstract" drawings, one with neatly traced, regular geometric forms, the other with sketchy, impulsive lines and dark strokes in asymmetric compositions. "Creative" personalities preferred the latter. This set looked pictorial and contained dozens of rapidly drawn lines, while in the first set, preferred by subjects chosen at random, the drawings were meager with a few thin ruled lines rendering a single unit or segment of ornament in the center of the field. One would like to know how the subjects would have responded had they been offered drawings with regular elements in a balanced asymmetric composition as complex as that of the sketchy examples.

27 I have tried to characterize the individual artists in that spectrum of styles in an article, "The Younger American Painters of Today" in *The Listener*, London, Jan. 26, 1956—a talk for a B.B.C. program in December 1955 on the exhibition at the Tate Gallery.

28 They are reproduced in *Centennial*, 1971, pp. 153–56, nos. 71–74 (74 in color), and by Seuphor, pp. 381–82, nos. 285–91.

29 Mondrian had already intertwined the grids in his painting *New York City* (1942). It is reproduced in color by Seuphor, p. 183. In a late work of 1943 (ibid., p. 297), he has ingeniously inserted in a diamond field what appears to be an overlay of two grids formed by intersecting and intercepted rectangles in successive parallel planes in depth. This idea in both works was perhaps suggested by his use of tapes in planning a composition. For an example of his working procedure see the unfinished version of that picture (*No. 3*), illustrated in Seuphor, p. 299.